I Hear My Gate Slam
Chinese Poets Meeting and Parting

Translated by Taylor Stoehr

2007 : Pressed Wafer : Boston

Acknowledgments:

Some of these translations first appeared in
Agni, Blue Unicorn, Field, Harvard Review, Mandrake, Nimrod, Rhino, and *Sampan.*

ISBN-13: 978-0-9785156-2-1
ISBN-10: 0-9785156-2-5

Cover painting and ink drawings by the translator
typeslowly designed
Printed in Michigan by Cushing-Malloy, Inc.
Pressed Wafer / 9 Columbus Square / Boston, MA 02116

Table of Contents

To my friend Bob Couture
whose gate is always open

i
Voices at Dusk

WANG WEI

The Peaks of Chungnan

The peaks of Chungnan stretch east
from the capital down to the sea.

Look back, white clouds close the view,
ahead, nothing but green mist.

Over each divide the landscape shifts,
light and shadow restless in the valleys.

If you want a night's sleep in the human world,
call across the stream to the woodcutter.

Bramble Brook

White rocks break the surface of Bramble Brook,
red leaves flutter in the cold wind.

No trace of rain on the mountain path
but the bushes will give you a soaking.

Cottage at Chungnan Mountain

In my middle years I set out on the Way,
old age finds me still on the mountainside.

When I take it in my head to wander off
exploring the unknowable all by myself

I follow the stream up to the highest falls,
settle down here to watch the mists rising.

Sometimes I meet an old woodcutter on the path.
We talk and laugh and I forget to go home.

Returning to My Cottage

Faraway bells echo in the valley,
one by one the woodsmen are heading home.

White clouds at the summit still beckon me
but how dark and somber the mountain has become!

An evening breeze bends the water-rushes,
catkin fluff flying everywhere.

Far to the east new grass greens the marshes
but here it is dusk. I go in and bar the door.

To Secretary Su, Who Did Not Find Me
at Home

My cottage sits at the mouth of the valley,
tall trees circling a tumbledown village.

No one here to open the gate to you,
just a stony road back for your trouble.

Fishing boats ice-bound along the river bank,
campfires burning on the cold plain.

White clouds in the distant sky.
Faint bells. At night a gibbon's cry.

Reply to Chief Chang

In old age only serenity matters,
the heart cares nothing for the busy world.

Take heed, make no far-reaching plans.
As for wisdom, seek it in the grove.

Wind in the pines. I loosen my belt.
Mountain moon shining. I tune my lute.

No difference between success and failure
while the fisherman's song fills the cove.

LIU TSUNG-YÜAN

Snow Falling

Mountains so high not even a bird can pass.
No paths here, not even a footprint.

One old man sits fishing from a boat,
snow falling on his leafy cloak.

Liu Tsung-yüan

The Old Fisherman

The old fisherman passes the night under the cliff.
At dawn he boils river water on a fire of bamboo.

Before the sun has burned off the mist, he's vanished,
the slap of his oars echoing on the mountainside.

Look to the horizon — there's his mast out in the current.
High above the cliff, lazy clouds sail across the sky.

LI PO

Sitting Alone at Jingting Mountain

Highflying flocks beat their way across the sky,
a single cloud lounges after them — gone!

Leaving us all alone,
Jingting Mountain and I.

In the Mountains

You want to know why I live here on the mountain?
Ha! What can I say? Is this where I am?

Peach blossoms reflected in the water —
in which green world do they bloom?

Visiting the Hermit Monk

Barking dogs and the sound of water,
peach blossoms heavy with dew.

Deer glimpsed deep in the forest,
noon bell too far away to hear.

Clumps of bamboo cleave the mist,
from the cliffs a cascade hangs in midair.

No one seems to know where he's gone —
I slouch moodily among the pines.

TU FU

Gazing at T'ai-Shan Mountain

How to tell you about T'ai-Shan?
Inexhaustible green from Ch'i to Lu.

Earthly beauty gathered to the sky,
Yin and Yang, dusk and dawn.

You gasp for breath at cloud-level,
wide-eyed as birds vanish and reappear.

Climb all the way to the top,
watch other mountains grow small.

Two Orioles

Two bright orioles warble
        in the green willows,
a line of white egrets stretches
        across the blue sky.

A thousand winters are piled on the peaks
        framed by my west window,
the boat from Wu, a thousand miles east,
        rides at anchor by my door.

I Wait Here Alone

Two white gulls glide to and fro.
High above them a hawk hovers.

Blind to the shadow flitting below,
they ride the wind along the river.

Morning dew drenches the grass.
The spider's web stretches wide.

The world attends to its business
of slaughter. I wait here alone.

PO CHÜ-I

Night Rain

The first cricket chirps once. Then again.
The lamp begins to flare and gutter.

Out in the dark it starts to rain,
the banana tree adds its tap and patter.

The Demon Poetry

I strive to pass through the Empty Gate
and clear my head of all its idle song,

but the Demon Poetry lies in wait:
a breeze, a moonbeam — I'm humming along.

Ask Yang Qiong

The ancients sang because their hearts were full,
today people sing just for the squeal.

If you want to know why, don't ask me,
go ask Yang Qiong the singsong girl.

HAN SHAN

Coming Home to Cold Mountain

Thirty years I've lived in this world,
thousands of miles I've traveled,

from river banks lush with green grass
to the red desert out beyond the pass.

I've dabbled in medicine and magic,
written poems, read the classics.

Now I've come home to Cold Mountain
to wash out my ears in the stream.

Too Many Words

Talking about food doesn't fill you up,
talking about clothes won't keep you warm.

What your belly wants is rice
and a thick coat is nice in a storm.

Sometimes words just confuse things
and make the Buddha hard to find.

While you're talking the Buddha sits
fat and warm inside your mind.

Book Learning

Book learning won't keep you from dying.
Book learning won't help you in hard times.

So why does anyone bother?
Because books lift you out of your rut.

If you grow up not knowing how to read,
you'll see nothing but the muddy road.

If you fail to sauce your supper of wild herbs,
don't be surprised to find them bitter.

A Bad Reputation

I used to carry a book along with my hoe,
back when I lived with my older brother.

I got a bad reputation that way,
even my wife thought me peculiar.

So I no longer dig in the red dust
but wander about and read as I wish.

You stranger, will you pour a dipper
for a poor fish flopping in the ditch?

My Cloak

I own but a single cloak,
neither of gauze nor fancy silk.

What color is it then? Well,
not scarlet and not purple.

In summer it's my sleaveless shirt,
in winter my quilted jacket.

Summer and winter turn about,
year after year won't wear it out.

What Counts

When some clever chap says to Cold Mountain,
"Your poems, my friend, are nonsense,"

I tell him, "Read the ancients!
For them, being poor was no disgrace."

But he just thinks it's funny
how daft Cold Mountain has gone.

"Nowadays, sir, everyone knows
nothing counts but money."

Life in a Bowl

Man lives in a circle of dust
like a beetle in a bowl,

busily going round and round
never getting anywhere.

Enlightenment never comes
to those who scrabble in the dirt.

Days flow by like the rushing river,
suddenly we find ourselves old.

Puzzling Things Out

Is my body real or just an illusion?
Who is it who asks such a question?

See how one puzzle leads to another!
I sit on the mountainside lost in wonder

till the green grass grows up between my toes
and the red dust settles on my head.

Country folk come to me with wine and fruit,
pious offerings set out for the dead.

Han Shan

Cold Mountain's Poems

Here are Cold Mountain's poems,
better medicine than pills or sutras.

Copy out your favorite
and pin it to the wall.

ii
Friends Meeting and Parting

MENG HAO-JAN, WANG WEI & LI PO

Farewell Advice to Meng Hao-jan

Shut the gate, stop up your ears,
turn your back on worldly cares.

Old friend, take my advice,
pack your bags at once!

A merry song, plenty of home-brew,
reciting the classics by heart —

That's the life for men like you,
let others bend their knees at court.

— *Wang Wei*

Saying Goodbye to Wang Wei

No will of my own, I delay
my departure day after day.

Yes, meadow grass smells sweet to me
but I miss your voice already.

Would the emperor relent
if he heard my lament?

Only silence and solitude wait
in my old garden behind the gate.

— *Meng Hao-jan*

Parting

We've said farewell on the mountainside,
day turns to night, my door of thatch is shut.

Grass will be green again in spring.
Old friend – will you come back or not?

— *Wang Wei*

Empty Window

No longer prostrate at the palace gate,
but back in my hut on the mountainside.

Without talent, ill, and all but friendless,
how was I to win the emperor's notice?

My hair's gone white, I'm getting old.
Green leaves fall fast when the sun's in decline.

Wide awake all night at the empty window,
I brood like moonlight on the shadowy pine.

— *Meng Hao-jan*

For Meng Hao-jan

I love my master Meng Hao-jan,
famed for his fancy, wild as the wind.

The rosy youth who tossed
aside the cap of office

now rests his head, snow white,
where mountain pine meets cloud.

Moon-drunk he lost his place,
flower-fuddled found the path.

Who can hope to rise so high?—
I bow to his pure spirit.

— Li Po

Meng Hao-jan, Wang Wei & Li Po

Birds at Sunrise

Slept right through sunrise —
birdsong fills the skies.

After last night's wild rain
how many petals must have fallen!

— Meng Hao-jan

Birds at Nightfall

Nose in a wine-cup I missed nightfall.
Every fold of my robe showers petals

as I shake off my moonlight spree.
All the birds have vanished — no one left but me.

— Li Po

Seeing Meng Hao-jan Off at Yellow Crane Tower

My old friend leaves the West
at Yellow Crane Tower.

April blossoms loom in the mist
as he floats off to Gwang-ling.

His sail a distant shadow
vanishing in the blue,

nothing left but the Long River
on its way to the sky.

— Li Po

Seeing a Friend Off

You dismount for a last cup of wine,
again I ask you where you're headed.

You say you're not happy here,
You'd rather be lying on your back at South Hill.

Go then! No more questions!
Seek your boundless white clouds.

— *Wang Wei*

Night on the Great River

Sundown: steering for shore through mist,
reluctant to tie up for another long night.

Trees dark and distant under enormous skies,
suddenly everything brightens, looms near: Moonrise.

— *Meng Hao-jan*

Weeping for Meng Hao-jan

I will not see my old friend on this visit,
only the River Han flowing ever east.

In Hsiang-yang I ask for him in vain,
all is silent on Deer Gate Mountain.

— *Wang Wei*

WANG WEI AND P'EI TI

Deer Park

No one to be seen on the mountain,
only voices echoing at dusk.

Late sun angling through the trees
lights up bluegreen lichen.

— Wang Wei

All day on the cold mountain
travelers come and go,

seeing nothing in the pine
but tracks of buck and doe.

—P'ei Ti

Bamboo Grove

Off by myself in the darkening grove,
plucking my lute and whistling along.

No one knows I'm here in the bamboo
where the bright moon also comes shining.

— Wang Wei

I come to the Bamboo Grove
to find the true Way,

mountain birds for company,
far from the world of men.

— P'ei Ti

Luan Rapids

Tempestuous autumn downpour,
runoff sluicing rock and stone,

rain into spray, splatter lost in splash —
a startled egret rises up, drops back down.

— *Wang Wei*

Far-off roar of rapids
as we near the South Ford.

Ducks and gulls rush
to investigate us.

— *P'ei Ti*

Hibiscus

Hibiscus flowering twig and tip,
the whole mountainside aflame.

By the stream a hut, silent and empty,
and petals falling as fast as they bloom.

— Wang Wei

Green banks lush with spring grass.
The princely recluse

loses himself in magnolias
and red hibiscus.

— P'ei Ti

Lake Yi

A flute sounds from the distant shore.
We say goodbye at sunset

and I row back across the lake.
The green cliffs vanish in mist.

— Wang Wei

Spreading wide and empty —
blue water, azure sky.

Boat moored, I whistle a tune
to the answering breeze.

— P'ei Ti

Caught in the Rain

Hard rain hides the bend in the river,
no gleam where water wets the sand.

The Wang winds its misty way along,
but where have the Chungnan Mountains gone?

— *P'ei Ti*

River rising, current cold and deep.
Autumn rain darkens the heavens.

You ask about the Chungnan Mountains —
look in your heart behind the billowing clouds!

— *Wang Wei*

LI PO AND TU FU

To a Friend Going Off to Shu

Everyone knows the Szechuan Road
is hard-going and full of surprises.
Mountains spring up in your face,
clouds swirl round your horse's head.

Heavy-scented boughs keep you ducking on
        the plank-path,
floods and freshets swamp the walls of Shu.
But these ups and downs will be in plain view,
no need to consult a diviner before setting forth.

— Li Po

Heartache Pavilion

In all the world this place is named most truly,
Heartache Pavilion, where friends say goodbye.

March winds blow bitterly here
where the willow fights back its green tears.

— *Li Po*

Taking Leave of a Friend

Blue mountains spread north of the city,
the white river hugs its eastern wall.
Once more you leave me at this place —
Ah! tumbleweed, you've many miles to travel!

Pale clouds pass over your wayfarer's face
as the sun sinks low in your old friend's heart.
We say good-bye, this is where we part.
Your horse whinnies once, twice. You ride away.

— *Li Po*

No News of Li Po

I've not seen Master Li lately
but he's still pursuing his folly.
Though people may gossip about him
he's higher than ever in my esteem.

A thousand sprightly stanzas
on the road between glasses!
He wrote his first poems near here —
not such a bad place to retire.

— *Tu Fu*

At Sand Hill City

Why have I come here to Sand Hill?
I do nothing all day long
but loiter near the city wall
where ancient trees sing their autumn song.

I can't get drunk on the wine of Lu,
the music of Ch'i leaves me down in the mouth.
All my thoughts flow toward you,
like the River Wen rushing south.

— *Li Po*

Dreaming of Li Po

Mourning for the dead may bring relief
but tears of exile have no end.
Such is the no-man's-land of grief,
waiting for news of a banished friend.

I brood on his fate all day,
at night he comes while I'm dreaming
though caged a thousand miles away —
old friend, you've taken wing!

Or am I haunted by your ghost?
Sunny groves, dark waters, forbidding heights,
surely too far even for your eagle spirit
to circle in a single night.

Moonlight floods my chamber,
your face brightens, is gone,
and the sea churns again. Beware
the claws of the water-dragon!

— *Tu Fu*

Spring Day: Thinking of Li Po

Master Li has no peer,
his poems leap and soar,
bold and free as Pao Chao,
as Yü Hsin fresh and clear.

It's Spring here north of the Wei,
all the trees in flower;
east of the Yangtze you watch
evening clouds appear.

Isn't it time for us to share
a jar of wine once more,
drunk on poetry,
forgetful of season and hour?

— *Tu Fu*

The Guest

Spring freshets on every side,
my only visitors are gulls.
Garden path deep in petals,
my gate swings wide — it's you!

Market far and coins few,
if you don't mind country fare
let's call on the old boy next door
and finish off his homebrew.

— *Tu Fu*

Meeting Tu Fu

Who should I run into
on Boiled Rice Mountain
but old Tu Fu
wearing a big bamboo hat

in the hot noonday sun.
How long it's been
since last we met!
But you look so thin —

what's eating you,
too much poetry?

— *attributed to Li Po*

PO CHÜ-I AND YÜAN CHEN

Azalea Inn

Coming and going on the same road,
      never the same day,
back and forth, each thinking of the other,
      wondering where he's gone.

Three or four miles beyond the gates
      of the highest pass,
on the wall at Azalea Inn
      I find your poem pinned.

— *Po Chü-i*

Dreaming of Yüan Chen

I arise at dawn for a breath of air,
      spirits strangely troubled.
Many rivers and streams lie between us,
      no news for a long time.

Tell me please, were you thinking
      of me last night,
in the middle of the third watch,
      when you appeared in my dream?

— *Po Chü-i*

Po Chü-i and Yüan Chen

Thanking Po Chü-i for Dreaming of Me

A thousand mountains between us,
      no news gets through.
Worried about my health,
      you see me in dreams.

Though my illness has passed
      my soul is still afflicted:
I dream only of nobodies,
      almost never of you.

— *Yüan Chen*

Reading Yüan Chen's Poems

I spread the scroll next to
      the lamp and read your poems,
finishing just before dawn.
      The wick has burned low

and my eyes ache. I blow it out
      and sit here in the dark,
listening to the waves beat
      against the windward bow.

— *Po Chü-i*

I Too Am Sleepless

Moored on the western bank
    you chanted my poems the whole night through;
here on the mountainside I too am sleepless —
    wind and rain and the call of the cuckoo.

— *Yüan Chen*

Late Spring

In the evening swallows
        appear at the window;
on my doorstep sparrows
        flutter in the dust.

At sundown a breeze stirs
        and I hear my gate slam;
a few petals fall silently
        but no one has come.

— *Yüan Chen*

iii
Woe to the Soldiers

What Grass Is Not Thirsty?

What grass is not thirsty?
　　　　what day with no muster?

Rounding up soldiers
　　　　to guard the frontier!

What grass never withers?
　　　　what man is not taken?

Woe to the soldiers,
　　　　once they were men!

Foxes and vixen
　　　　skulk in the bracken,

tiger and buffalo,
　　　　sharp hoof and claw.

The war chariot rolls
　　　　down desolate trails.

Woe to the soldiers,
　　　　once they were men!

— Book of Songs (800 – 600 B.C.E.)

Joined Up at Fifteen

Joined up at fifteen,
at eighty I've served my time.
A fellow I met near home
answered all my questions
by pointing to tombs
under the pines.

The cottage roof has fallen,
pheasants roost on the crossbeam,
rabbits use old dogholes to get in.
Wild grain has sprouted in the yard
and mallow chokes the well.

I'd harvest some grain to boil,
add mallow to the pail
for soup, bivouac style,
but who would share my meal?

I stare out the Eastern portal
while hot tears fall.

> — *Anon (from the Yueh-fu,*
> *Western Han, 206 B.C.E. – 8 C.E.)*

Frontier Soil

Has there ever been a time without war,
       an emperor without armies?

Soldiers have but one thing on their minds,
       the lookout for peace.

At the frontier they say the soil now
       is more bones than earth,

poor farmers dragged from their fields
       and marched off to death.

— Wei Chuang

Ballad of the Army Wagons

Wagons rumbling, horses whinnying,
soldiers with bow and arrow swinging at their belts.
Running after them fathers mothers wives children,
saying goodbye at Hsiang-Yang Bridge.

The soldiers disappear in a cloud of dust.
Their families are left crowding the roadway,
rending their garments and stamping their feet.
Their lamentations rise to the very heavens.

A traveler myself, I stopped a soldier
as they marched by, and this was his story:

We went north at fifteen
to defend the Yellow River,
they're calling us up at forty
for the forts out west.

When we left, our village elders
had to tie our headbands for us.
We've come back with grey hair
to what? — another tour of duty!

The frontiers run with blood
while our own villages go
back to briars and brambles.
The Emperor thinks only of conquest.

Even if there's a wife to plow
the furrows run every which way.
And how do they welcome old soldiers in Ch'in?
They drive us like dogs or chickens!

The last levy of troops isn't back
but already the District Officers
demand the grain tax.
Where is it supposed to come from?

These days the birth of a son is a disaster!
You're lucky if you have a girl —
at least she can marry out of the family.
You might as well bury a son in the pasture.

The faraway shores of the Kokonor
are strewn with unburied bones.
The newly dead wail and ancient spirits weep
under dark and drizzling skies.
Their voices twitter like birds at twilight.

—*Tu Fu*

The Farmer

His water buffalo bellows a complaint.
Soil baked hard and cracked like a broken plate,
the clods explode under its hooves.

Plowing his field for the Emperor,
sixty years he's watched the wagons rolling off
to feed the soldiers God knows where!

Then one day government troops come
to slaughter his buffalo and take away his cart.
They leave him two buffalo horns.

He hammers the ploughshare into a spade,
while his wife hauls his sister threshes
for without grain for taxes he must sell his house.

We pray for victory. Though the farmer will die
he has an heir, and the buffalo a calf.
Supplies for the army must never run short!

— *Yüan Chen*

The Great Wall

Year after year we man the border;
it takes many soldiers to secure
the Great Wall against Mao Tun
and his barbarian horsemen.

We spent a fortune building it
high enough to repel a bandit;
but bandits have other ways to come,
the Great Wall doesn't stop the Hun.

Doubts arise when the young ask the old
whether the investment is solid.
Once when the Hun besieged the capital
didn't the Emperor flee his own city walls?

Now the Hun have sued for peace,
and we watch their troops riding away.
Not believing what they say,
we keep piling up mountains of defense.

It's not for me to pronounce on foreign policy
but here's a humble worker's opinion —
the strongest bulwark is diplomacy
if you want a wall to contain the Hun.

— *Yüan Chen*

The Grain Tax

The tax collector pounds at the gate
in the middle of the night
demanding grain before daylight —
out to the barn with candles and lamps!

The winnowed kernels shine like pearls,
thirty sacks loaded in the cart.
What if it's not enough? honest folk
cringing like slaves under the whip.

I myself once held office
it shames me now to say.
Four times I took my seat,
fed ten years at the trough.

Everyone knows the ancient wisdom —
The moon waxeth and waneth ever.
Perhaps the emperor will have a change of heart
and send back this year's tribute?

— *Po Chü-i*

The Old Charcoal-Seller

The old charcoal-seller
cuts his wood and fires it on South Hill.
A face the color of soot, all smoke and dust,
grizzled temples, ten fingers blacker than black,
he hawks his charcoal for the wherewithal
to hang a coat on his back and put food in his belly.

Alas, such a thin coat, and yet he prays
for cold weather to boost his sales.
Last night it snowed outside the city,
at dawn his cart was breaking ice in the ruts.
Bullock tired and driver hungry, sun high in the sky,
they come to a muddy stop at the Market Gate.

But then two elegant horsemen gallop up,
a yellow-robed official and servant in whitest white.
They unroll an imperial scroll and read it out,
turn the cart round, shout at the ox, and head north.
His cartload of charcoal, a thousand pounds,
is required at the palace immediately. There it goes.

Half a measure of red silk and a length of damask
will be tossed across the bullock's horns to pay for it.

— *Po Chü-i*

The Recruiting Officer

I had stopped for lodgings at Shih-hao.
That night a recruiting officer came for men.
One old fellow scrambled over the wall
while his wife was opening the gate.
How furiously the officer shouted at her!
The old woman just stood there weeping,
and I heard her speak these bitter words:

My three sons went to the fort at Yeh.
Already one has written to tell me
his two brothers have been killed.
For the time being he is alive
but his brothers are dead forever.
I have no more sons to give you.
My grandson is still at the breast,
are you going to draft his mother?
She hasn't even got a skirt to wear.
What about me, old and feeble as I am?
I beg you, sir, take me instead of them
to fill out your levy for Ho-yang.
I could cook rice for the soldiers …

Night closed in and the voices faded
except for what sounded like muffled sobs.
When I rose at dawn and went my way
only the old man was there to say farewell.

— *Tu Fu*

At the Western Pass

At the Western Pass, wind and sand,
leafless trees, yellowing grass.

From these barren heights our guards
keep watch for the Tartar foe.

Far below, a deserted fort commands the plain,
but not a wall of the old village stands.

Only bones, thousands of bones,
heaped and bleaching in the bracken.

Who is more to blame, the treacherous Tartar
or our emperor beside himself with rage?

Obedient armies beat the drums of war,
the sun goes dark, the air smells of blood.

Recruiting officers raid the countryside —
three-hundred-sixty thousand men!

Mid cries of woe and tears like rain
the doomed conscripts are marched off.

Who will plow the fields and dig the gardens
while our sons pace the bitter mountain pass?

Don't tell us how Li Mu once triumphed,
where soldiers have always been fed to wolves!

— Li Po

Night on the Citadel Walls

At the foot of Hui-le Mountain, the sand looks like snow.
Out beyond the walls, moonlight or frost?

Somewhere in the darkness a Tartar flute drones,
and all night long the soldiers dream of home.

— Li Yi

Fighting South of the Wall

Last year we fought where the Sang-kan flows,
this year it was Onion River Road.

We've washed our swords in the Eastern Sea,
grazed our horses on T'ien Shan's snowy side.

A thousand miles are not enough for this war,
our armies grow old in their armor.

Husbandmen of slaughter, the Huns
have sown the yellow desert with our bones.

Long ago the Ch'in built the Great Wall,
now it's the Han who light the signal-beacon.

All night long the flames flicker,
year in year out, the war goes on.

Bright swords flash, brave men fall and die,
riderless horses whinny at the sky.

Kites and crows pluck out the guts,
hang them high on the withered trees.

Soldiers smear their blood on the dry grass
while generals map the next campaign.

Wise men know winning a war
is no better than losing one.

—Li Po

Dispatches from the Front

A fresh horse every ten leagues,
whip swinging again after five,
the general's dispatches arrive:

Tartar troops surround Chin-ch'uan,
snow falling in the mountains,
beacon fires out, ominous sky.

— *Wang Wei*

At the Ford

Late autumn. I water my horse at the ford,
an icy draught, and wind like a knife.

Here to horizon there's nothing but sand,
and darkening in the distance — the Great Wall.

In ancient times fierce warriors
won everlasting glory in its shadow.

Yellow dust covers everything now;
here and there in the tumbleweed — bones.

— *Wang Ch'ang-ling*

Song of the Frontier

Sworn to sweep the Tartar border clean
      whatever the cost,

five thousand soldiers in their fur-trimmed finery
      died in the dust.

Pity their bones sleeping along the River
      of Restless Sands.

Pity their ghosts haunting the bedchambers
      of last Spring's brides.

— Ch'en Tao

Hunting Tigers

A shadow in the woods,
   wind stirring the grass;
our general draws his bow
   just as night comes down.

In the morning white feathers
   lead us to the arrow
buried deep in its quarry —
   a massive block of stone.

— Lu Lun

The King of Yüeh

When the King returned from the sacking of Wu
      his warriors rode home in rich brocades.
Courtly ladies filled the Spring Palace like flowers,
      where partridges now spread their wings.

— Li Po

The Summer Palace

In the desolate summer palace
        the peonies are still red
and white-haired palace ladies say what they please
        about the palace dead.

— *Yüan Chen*

Piling Up Glory

Alas for meadowland! Hill and stream
       crawling with armies!

How are plain folks to live,
       their fields and woods a war zone?

We're sick of your talk about heroes
       and famous victories,

some general piling up glory
       on thousands of rotting bones.

— Ts'ao Sung

Waiting for the Ambassador

Hemmed in by a wilderness of mountains,
the citadel lies halfway up an alpine vale.

Battlements loom in the foggy dawn,
above the pass the moon grows pale.

Our ambassador has gone to witness
the beheading of the rebel leader.

I've waited all night by the watchfire,
smoke in my eyes, cheeks like old leather.

— *Tu Fu*

Thinking of My Brothers on a Moonlit Night

Drums on the ramparts day and night,
travelers halted at the gates.

High above our frontier garrison
a wild goose heading south cries out.

Dew lies white on the cold ground,
the moon shines down as it does at home.

Letters no better than a stab in the dark
now that the war is raging again.

Anyway, all my brothers are gone,
none left to say who's alive, who's not.

— *Tu Fu*

from Journey to the North

From the rise I finally see Fu Chou
across the rolling hills and valleys.

I hurry down the path to the river bank,
my servant lagging behind in the line of trees.

Owls hoot from the darkening mulberry grove,
marmots raise their tiny paws like guardian deities.

At midnight we pass by an old battleground,
the cold moon shining down on white bones.

A thousand thousand warriors gathered at T'ung Pass,
half the population of mighty Ch'in.

How could so many perish at a single stroke,
cut down and sent tumbling to another life?

I too have rolled in the Tartar dust,
returning home with my hair snow white.

— *Tu Fu*

iv
Exile and Loneliness

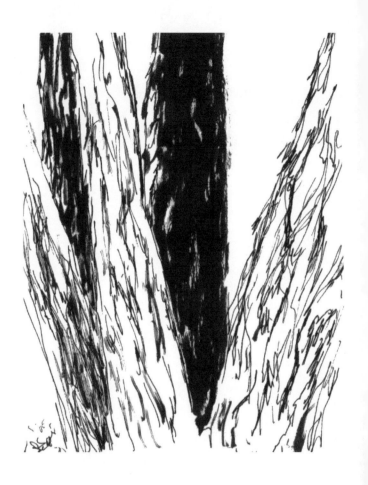

LIU TSUNG-YÜAN

Exile in Ch'u

I used to be trussed in red-tape, skewered by my hat-pin,
but now they've sent me packing to the backwoods.

I've plenty of time to putter in the garden, and brood,
indistinguishable from any other country bumpkin.

At sunrise you'll find me plowing in the morning dew,
at night hear my oars scraping along in the shallows.

Coming or going, there's no one to say hello.
I sing all day long under the blue sky of Ch'u.

Liu Tsung-yüan

Morning Walk

Autumn almost over, frost every morning now,
I take my usual stroll up the valley.

Across the bridge where the stream's gone yellow
with fallen leaves, an old village stands empty.

Nothing but a few cold flowers, an ancient tree,
and somewhere a fountain's faltering flow.

Suddenly all my gathered thoughts desert me —
in the woods something has startled a young doe.

HAN SHAN

Blinking at Shadows

Sat down once to gaze on Cold Mountain,
and here I've been sitting thirty years.

Went looking yesterday for family and friends,
but half have already gone to the Yellow Springs.

Life fades like a flickering candle,
hurries past like the ceaseless river.

This morning, blinking at shadows,
suddenly my eyes are filled with tears.

WANG WEI

Saying Goodbye at Wei City

At Wei City morning rain
        wets the dust,
a willow beside the inn
        is newly green.
Let's empty one last
        cup of wine
before you head west.
        You'll find
no old friends beyond
        the Yang Pass.

MENG HAO-JAN

Night Letter to the Gwang-ling Ramblers

Gibbons are wailing in the mountains
as the blue river rushes toward night.
A breeze sighs in the leaves along the banks,
and the moon shines down on one lone boat.

Jyen-de is surely no place for me.
Do you remember our rambles in Gwang-ling?
Think of them when you read these lines,
tears shed far from where the great sea rolls.

LIU CH'E

Fallen Leaves

Silk sleeves no longer rustle
in the jade courtyard, dust settles
in the empty room.

Fallen leaves collect against the double
barred doors as if to follow
after beauty gone.

Will longing never be done?

LI SHANG-YIN

Night Rain: a Letter to the North

You ask when I'll return
        but I don't know.
At Pa Shan night rain swells
        the autumn pools.

When will we trim the candle
        in the west window
whispering together of Pa Shan
        and its night rain?

LI PO

Jade Flute

In one of those dark houses
someone is playing a jade flute.

Music floats on the spring air,
filling the streets of Lo-yang.

When "The Broken Willow"
echoes in the still night,

who can listen without a pang,
who does not dream of home?

Sorrow

Beautiful face drawn back behind
      pearl-studded blinds.
Deep in shadow the pencilled brows
      frown like moth wings.

Nothing more is revealed,
      only the wet tracery of tears.
Unfathomable heart,
      dark and mysterious song.

Lines to an Ancient Tune

The forest spreads and swirls like mist
            across the wide plain.
On the mountainside a single belt
            of heart-breaking green.

Dusk descends on the high tower.
            Again the solitary watcher
has climbed jade steps in vain.

The darkening sky swarms with doves
            returning to their cote.
Near or far the next outpost
            lies no closer to home.

Setting Out Early

At dawn we leave the mountain citadel,
measure a thousand miles in one day's sail.

Gibbons scream from the river banks,
our mast glides past the countless peaks.

Thoughts on a Quiet Night

Awakened in bed by bright moonlight,
everything gleaming like frost,

I lift my head — where is it coming from?
Lie down again dreaming of home.

Ancient Airs No. 11

Yellow River racing east to the sea,
white sun sinking fast in the west.

Hastening current, melting light,
gone before you know it.

Spring has faded from my face,
mildew and frost blight my harvest.

If only I could stand firm
like some old wintry pine.

If not, let me vanish
riding the whirlwind, breathing fire.

TU FU

Spring Night at the Imperial Court

Shadowy blossoms on the wall at dusk,
birds go twittering to roost.

Stars shine down on ten thousand doors
and the moon has grown fat in the sky.

Wakeful, I listen for the bronze gates,
imagine bridle-bells on the wind.

In the morning I must present my scroll.
Watchman, I call again, how long till dawn?

Spring Scene

Imperial borders disintegrating,
only mountains and rivers remain.
In the city it must be Spring,
grass and trees lush again.

A spray of plum blossoms
brings tears to my eyes.
I've been in exile so long
every bird breaks my heart.

The beacon fires are lit
and burning now three months.
Just one letter from home
would be worth a pot of gold.

I've pulled and fretted
my white hair so thin
there's not enough left
to twist a top knot.

Another Spring

Birds whiter than white against the river's jade,
vermilion flowers on the mountainside.

Another Spring burning itself up.
When will it be my turn to set forth?

Traveling at Night

Along the grassy bank night breezes stir,
a lone mast stark against the sky.

Over the great river stars spread their canopy,
moonlight bobs in the current.

So much for poet's glory,
so much for the public man past his prime.

Adrift in an empty universe
one glaucous gull rides the dark waves.

An Old-Fashioned Belle

An old-fashioned belle
lives down this lane.
        Once the pride of her family
        now she droops and pines.

Our civil wars long ago
dealt her brothers death.
        High station laid them low,
        bones scattered on the path.

The world shuns misfortune,
fate's candle flickers in the wind.
        Her faithless husband has taken
        a new wife, flawless as jade.

The lowly vetch folds its leaves,
ducks settle down in pairs.
        The smiling face of new love
        laughs off old love's tears.

Clear water from a mountain spring
grows muddy in the river's rush.
> She sends her maid to sell her pearls,
> mends the thatch with vines and brush.

Instead of flowers for her hair
she gathers cypress boughs.
> Her blue sleeves thin against the cold,
> she lingers in the tall bamboo.

From a Height

Winds howl, the gibbons keen it back,
higher and higher soar the tireless gulls.

A thousand trees shed a thousand leaves,
down and down the hurrying river flows.

My wanderings this melancholy autumn
have brought me to a pause on these windy heights.

In the panorama of longing and regret
there is but one lesson — why so hard to learn?

PO CHÜ-I

To the Hermit Cheng

They tell me you have come
to live amongst these graves,
an old gatehouse your home,
deep in the bamboo groves.

I've followed to ask you
to lend me your garden
while you're gone, to use
for looking at the mountain.

Li Po's Grave

By Tsai-Shih River Li Po's grave.
Meadow grass underfoot and clouds above.

Here lies the glorious drunkard whose songs
vexed the court and made the gods laugh.

Every poet walks the same downhill path.
At the end, even you, a pile of bones.

from Old Age

My bed has been placed near a plain white screen,
the stove moved closer to the blue curtain.

I listen to my grandchildren reading,
watch the servant boy heat up my soup.

I exchange little poems with friends,
pawn an old gown for medicine.

And when I tire of this trifling,
I'll lie back in the sun and sleep.

Afterword: Translating Classical Chinese Poetry

Some people say that poetry isn't really translatable. The sounds and characters of one language have no genuine equivalents in any other, and the thoughts and feelings of a culture can only be understood by its natives. Obviously there is truth in this view, but if the language barrier were absolutely impenetrable, the world would be a prison of words. As with our bodies, we all use language to reach out to others, and translation is another way to embrace the unfamiliar, bringing people closer and fostering bonds of friendship. What is necessary is a leap of the imagination into the spirit of another person, and that is not merely a matter of finding word-matches between two languages. In the case of translation, it certainly helps to be a skilled writer, but even more crucial are ordinary human impulses like curiosity, admiration, and compassion. Ezra Pound and Kenneth Rexroth might not read Classical Chinese, but with some help from those who could, they created new works alive with the poetic spirit of Li Po and Tu Fu.

Both the difficulties of bridging the language barrier and the possibility of doing so are illustrated by the fact that even literal, word-for-word translations by bilingual native speakers often differ, since Chinese characters have several meanings and many nuances, all the more so in a poem. Consider, for example, the lines by Wang Wei that I have entitled "Deer Park." The scholar and translator Burton Watson provides the following modern Mandarin transcription, in Wade-Giles romanization—

> Kung shan pu chien jen
> tan wen jen yü hsian
> fan yin ju shen lin
> fu chao ch'ing t'ai shang

then a literal translation—

> Empty mountain not see man
> only hear man talk sound
> return light enter deep wood
> again shine green moss on

and finally his own poetic version—

> Empty hills, no one in sight,
> only the sound of someone talking;
> late sunlight enters the deep wood,
> shining over the green moss again.

Watson titles the poem "Deer Fence." Another scholar calls it "Deer Enclosure" and a third offers "Deer Park," a choice that fits my own sense of Wang Wei's meaning. In English "fence" and "enclosure" suggest trapped animals, whereas this secluded spot on Wang Wei's estate probably had its name because deer were often to be found there, not because they were kept there like pets or cattle. The various Chinese linguists who have translated the poem may agree on most of its words, but there are significant differences like this one.

Looking at the sequence of five words in the first line of Watson's literal version, an English reader should be able to gather its basic import, since word-order functions more or less the same way in Chinese that it does in English. Yet the line may seem syntactically crude, if not a bit cryptic to English readers. There isn't enough information. Chinese readers have the opposite problem with English texts. They are confused by too many "unnecessary" words — pronouns, articles, prepositions, auxiliary verbs marking tenses — which are the rule in English.

If we supply such words, one step beyond the literal translation, the line becomes a simple English sentence —

> [on the] empty mountain [one does] not see [a] person

This reading makes more sense than some other alternatives, like this one —

> [the] empty mountain [does] not see [a] person

Most of the lines in this poem provide semantic clues to their syntactic underpinning, and once there is more than the bare literal sequence on the translator's page, the poet's idea begins to emerge. Although dependent on particular words and unique sentences, poetic meaning is richer than the matter-of-fact utterance — a heightened experience calling upon the imagination. Sometimes it comes in a flash — the poem is saying *this* to me. We can think of it as a more intense version of the reaching out we make whenever we converse, trying to explain ourselves or understand each other — nothing esoteric, but more profoundly experienced than ordinary speech.

I think we begin to approach the deeper levels of Wang Wei's poem when we notice that the deer of his title never appear, are never even mentioned. Reading an answering poem from his friend P'ei Ti, who was much more plain-spoken than Wang himself, we find the illusive deer "present" as tracks in the forest. For P'ei Ti they exist by implication —

> seeing nothing in the pine
> but tracks of buck and doe.

P'ei Ti has understood that his friend's poem poses a paradox of presence and absence. Consider, for instance, the whereabouts of other people in Wang Wei's first couplet —

> No one to be seen on the mountain,
> only voices echoing at dusk.

People are not there, but their voices tell us so, reminding us of their absence. It's rather like the child, up to some mischief, who hears mother humming softly in the next room, and is thereby reassured that she is not in *this* room. In the case of the child, the *absence* of the presence is the important thing. An example closer to Wang Wei's meaning would be the memory of a loved one who has left or died, a very familiar theme in Classical Chinese poetry. The bereft poet is constantly in the *presence* of absence — an empty place at the family table, an empty bed — so that the ache of loss seems never to go away.

> Silk sleeves no longer rustle
> in the jade courtyard, dust settles
> in the empty room. (*Liu Ch'e*)

No one has vanished or died in Wang Wei's poem, but there is a strong sense of the nowhereness of the others whose voices can be heard. I want to call this "the presence of the absence" — absent friends and loved ones hovering in the imagination.

This paradoxical idea of a present absence is taken up again in Wang Wei's second couplet, where the visual effect of sunlight slanting through the trees is similar to the auditory effect of voices in the first couplet. The sun itself cannot be seen, but it is present in the brightness that lights up objects in view. Perhaps we can savor Wang Wei's meaning more fully if we consider several literal translations in addition to

Watson's. Their different versions of one line clarify the attitude I find behind the entire poem—

> return light enter deep wood
> (*Burton Watson*)
>
> reflecting shadow enter deep forest
> (*Wai-lim Yip*)
>
> returning sunlight enters deep forest
> (*Greg Whincup*)
>
> return shadow/light enter deep forest
> (*Hugh Stimson*)

Notice that the second Chinese character, *ying*, can be translated by the English words "light," "shadow," or "sunlight." The Chinese embraces all these possibilities. Light and shadow are understood in a reciprocal relation, similar to hot and cold, or more exactly, here and there—the one blotting out the other while also mirroring it. Wang Wei's poem invites us to see in our imagination both the shadows of the trees in late afternoon and also the light upon them, which illuminates their surfaces. The sun is implied by both shadow and light. The immediate impression conveyed is the sense of utter solitude, lit up by traces of what is not there.

At the same time, this solitude highlights all the more vividly what *is* there. This paradox is a characteristic effect of much of Wang Wei's poetry, his deep-going Buddhist apprehension of the universe, full of illusion and reality. His precise spiritual attitude — a Buddhist might call it lingering at the Empty Gate — is what I must learn when I try to find the right words in English. Finding my own words for Wang Wei's thought brings it closer, makes it my thought too. The effort to understand others helps us know ourselves.

It is particularly gratifying to translate T'ang Dynasty poets like Wang Wei, Tu Fu, and Li Po, because there are so many instances of close friendship among them. They often wrote poems borrowing, imitating, or otherwise reflecting each other's work. The *Wang River Sequence* of Wang Wei and P'ei Ti was an unusually elaborate result of a practice that was very common. Poetic exchanges in those times were more than mere letters written to absent friends. They were like duets harmonized at great distances, meant to draw the absent friend close in the imagination. And by echoing a friend's poem, these artists were also opening their hearts to currents of the wider universe of human thought and feeling. Indeed, that is one way to understand their passion for the classics, their love of allusion, quotation, and imitation. Often isolated or in exile, they felt the pang of loss and loneliness that every thinking person experiences at times. They did not deny their longing, but shared it and thereby gave one another solace and hope. The translator a thousand years later also hopes for a portion of the same comfort.

Notes

MENG HAO-JAN AND HIS FRIENDS,
WANG WEI AND LI PO

Wang Wei had many poet friends, including Li Po, the only poet of his generation whose ease and brilliance could be said to equal that of Wang. Born the same year, in 701, Wang and Li were both admirers of Meng Hao-jan, who was a dozen years older and lived a rather different life — one they sometimes seemed to envy. Unlike his two friends, Meng was never successful at court. After a youth spent quietly, writing and enjoying life in the country, Meng decided at forty to try his luck at the capital. It was in Ch'ang-an where he first met Wang Wei, just embarked on his own precocious career. One story has it that Meng was visiting Wang in his office when the emperor suddenly arrived. Meng hid under a couch, but the emperor spotted him and even seemed to know who he was. He requested a poem, throwing Meng into confusion. He recited a poem not unlike one of those I have translated — complaining of his lack of preferment. What! cried the emperor, much annoyed at the suggestion that he had denied Meng's suit. You have never approached me for my patronage!

Perhaps it was true, as Li Po suggests in one of his poems, that Meng chose his fate. In any case, he left the capital with ambivalence. Although not really suited to official life, he would miss his poet friends. It is probably significant that among the three poets, Meng seems to be the one most often lamented and lamenting, although the vicissitudes of public life caused much more hardship for Wang Wei and Li Po. I have included two poems Meng wrote that are not addressed to Wang Wei or Li Po, to illustrate his moody spirit more fully.

WANG WEI AND P'EI TI: A POETIC FRIENDSHIP

There are many remarkable friendships recorded among poets, but few have so unusual a story behind them as that between Wang Wei, one of the most famous of the great T'ang Dynasty poets of the Eighth Century, and his lesser known friend P'ei Ti. During the An Lu-shan Rebellion that ravaged China in his day, Wang Wei was captured and imprisoned along with many members of the Emperor's Court. P'ei Ti risked his own freedom to visit Wang Wei in prison, where they discussed the martyrdom of one of the court musicians who had resisted rebel demands for service. Wang Wei, himself a musician, was so moved that he immediately wrote a poem on the subject, which was smuggled out of the prison by P'ei Ti. But Wang Wei did not possess such bravery himself, and reluctantly he served the rebel court. After the Emperor eventually crushed the rebellion, all those who had gone over to the rebels were punished. Wang Wei was accused of treason, but his loyalty was attested by his poem, which had circulated widely during the interim regime thanks to P'ei Ti. Poetry and friendship saved Wang's life.

Wang Wei's paintings were as widely admired as his poems, but none of them survive — only the vivid landscapes he painted in verse. His most famous poetic rendering of the natural world was undertaken in collaboration with his friend P'ei Ti. For their *Wang River Sequence* each poet composed twenty poems describing their favorite walks together on Wang Wei's country estate. Wang Wei would write his four lines first, then P'ei Ti responded with his own picture-in-words, borrowing motifs from his friend's rendering. I have translated five of these dialogues, and a sixth in which P'ei Ti sets the task and Wang Wei replies.

LI PO AND TU FU

When they first met in 742 AD, Li Po was already a famous poet, Tu Fu just a beginner. Given the difference of eleven years in their ages, it was natural that most of the poems passed between them would come from Tu Fu, who was not only younger but also took life's ups and downs much more to heart. In their friendship over many years, both poets were often on the road or posted in distant provinces, parted by war and exile, and yet except for two poems written at the beginning of their acquaintance, it was always Tu Fu who wrote the lines of farewell. Li Po's half of their conversation has been lost, if it ever existed, so I've added here a few farewell poems Li Po might have addressed to Tu Fu, but probably wrote to someone else.

To fill out my imagined portrait of their friendship, I have included one jolly poem not by Li Po although traditionally attributed to him, and another by Tu Fu ("The Guest") which was not addressed to Li Po. This boisterous tone can be found in their other writings, especially those of Li Po, though the extant poems addressed by Tu Fu to Li Po are more often wry than exuberant.

PO CHÜ-I AND YÜAN CHEN

In a time of notable friendships, the most celebrated of all was that of Po Chü-i and Yüan Chen. From the time they were young officials, both assigned to duties in the Palace Library, till the death of Yüan some thirty years later, they relied on one another for inspiration and moral support. Because they were talented and dedicated to the public good, their careers were full of ups and downs. They were in or out of favor every few years, Yüan Chen in exile, Po serving in minor posts faraway, then both suddenly recalled to the capital by a new regime. All in all they lived in the same city for less than half a dozen years, but managed to keep their long friendship alive by means of numberless poems. Along with the usual songs of loss and loneliness, Po and Yüan, especially the latter, were able to regard their separations with humor and irony as well as pathos. Perhaps this is what made their writings so popular. In any case, their friendship became "a sort of national institution," as Arthur

Waley put it in his biography of Po Chü-i. According to Waley, they "were identified in people's minds as though they were one person," and when they met in 823, after one of their many long separations, it is said that people crowded the streets of Hangchow to see them walk together once more.

WOE TO THE SOLDIERS

The social distance between high officials and common people was very great in the China of 1000 years ago, and yet it was not unlikely that someone like Tu Fu or Po Chü-i, traveling on government business, would have contact and conversation with an aged farm wife, or a peasant conscript on his way to an army post at the frontier. In our own day important people always travel "first class," but in those times rich and poor might rub shoulders on the only road there was.

Whether or not poems like "The Recruiting Officer" or "The Ballad of the Army Wagons" report actual encounters, Tu Fu clearly meant them to sound like true stories of what people said and did in his presence. Much of the poignancy of these poems comes from this combination of personal immediacy and social distance, the pathos of poverty witnessed across the gulf of class and power by the poet on his own precarious journey through uncertain times.

The stability of empire was rarely secure; factionalism and power struggles within the court made the life of a poet-official almost as chancy as that of a poor farmer. But state power, like every major burden of life and livelihood in ancient China, fell most heavily on the shoulders of the peasant farmer, in the forms of taxation and war. Among the concerns of many poets of that time are poverty and injustice, the miseries of the soldier's life, the delusions of empire and the war spirit. Po Chü-i once wrote, "The duty of literature is to be of service to the writer's generation; that of poetry to influence public affairs" — sounding like Shelley in Waley's translation. These challenges are all the more to the point in our own day, though the imagery may be dated: desert forts, mountain ramparts, the Great Wall, and scattered everywhere, bones. I leave the reader to supply modern equivalents.